Sjoerd de Waal

LEAD BETWEEN THE LINES

Sjoerd de Waal

Trainnovator
+31(0)628149402
sjoerd@trainnovation.nl
TRAINNOVATION- *Growing by Sharing*

www.leadbetweenthelines.com
book@leadbetweenthelines.com

Second Edition, October 2015
First published in 2014
ISBN: 978-1-77277-003-2

Contents

Foreword

You thought it was easy, didn't you? Becoming a leader was your ultimate goal for years and now you have finally made it. But what a disappointment it is. You had never thought it to be so stressful. You weren't prepared for this.

Like millions of other leaders across the world, you have been very good at the job you've had for years. But now you need different skills and competencies.

With "Lead Between the Lines", Sjoerd de Waal guides you through this, for you, new and confusing territory called leadership. Using his powerful model, "The House of Leadership" he takes you by the hand and shows you where to pay attention.

You will learn to build your leadership on a strong foundation, called awareness. Awareness of where you stand in your organisation, not only as a leader, but also as a follower and a peer.

From this foundation, you will develop your skills in communication, goals, execution and learning. These four pillars will support your roof of trust.

Sjoerd de Waal has trained, coached and mentored numerous leaders in different positions, ranging from newbie to seasoned. After 25 years of practising and studying leadership, he now shares his wealth of practical knowledge with you.

Lead Between the Lines is written in a pleasant style and will surely help you Stop Suffering, Start Leading and Get results Now!

I surely hope you will enjoy reading this book as much as I did and I wish you all the success in your career as a leader. With this book, you can already take a giant step forward!

Raymond Aaron,
New York Times Bestselling Author.

P.S.: Have you noticed that Sjoerd also has some irresistible bonuses ready for you? In the book he explains how you can obtain them.

Introduction

Ever since I have started managing and leading, now about twenty-five years ago, I wanted to know more about how people lead.

While going through the ranks, it struck me that so few managers actually understood how to do it. That was true for myself as well.

At a certain point in my career I was responsible for a department of about twenty-five employees. It was at the turn of the century. I did not only feel responsible for those twenty-five, but also for their families. If I would mess up, they would suffer as well.

At that point, I decided to go to university and study for an MBA degree. I wanted to strengthen my foundation of awareness and improve my leadership skills.

I have not only learned a lot of theory, but also much about how to interact as a leader. In 2003 I got my MBA. It gave my career a boost, but my hunger for knowledge had not been satisfied. I kept on learning, reading and practising. It still strikes me that even nowadays so many leaders or managers don't know how to lead properly.

According to Gallup's 2013 report, "State of the global workplace", only 13% of employees across 142 countries worldwide are engaged in their job. You can imagine the consequences.

They also found that one of the major contributors to this low engagement is poor management. Hiring the wrong leaders or not coaching them the right way. People disengage because of bad leadership from their direct leader.

For more information on this very interesting report, visit: http://www.gallup.com/strategicconsulting/164735/state-global-workplace.aspx

With Lead Between the Lines I want to help you become a better leader, who understands what's needed to engage the people he leads.

Through my coaching and training I have already helped many leaders to improve their leadership. With this book I want to reach more leaders worldwide, so that they can improve on their leadership as well and get more employees feel engaged at work. This will also increase their joy in leadership.

Make the world a better place by sharing your improved leadership. Enjoy reading Lead Between the Lines!

Sjoerd de Waal
©2014

Chapter 1 - What did I do to deserve this?

Congratulations! You have made it! Finally you are a leader. You have stared at the greener grass of leadership for a long time now and it was about time that they recognised your skills and competencies. You're about to show them how to lead.

Maybe you already have experienced that excelling at your job as a specialist is something completely different from being a leader. You need a very different set of skills. But don't worry, you're about to learn what those skills are. I promise you.

Learning to lead takes time, a lot of time and you must be absolutely sure that you want to be a leader. Why? Because you will encounter many challenges, some of which may be overwhelming and challenge your moral.

It's a very demanding job, but also very rewarding. I don't mean the money, but the satisfaction when you see the results of your efforts.

If you don't want to put in the extra effort to become a great leader, you'd better stop reading. If you do want to put in that extra effort, which by the way I think is the case, since you have made the first step and opened this book, then please continue with this book and enjoy the ride!

Which skills brought you here?

Yes, in all probability you excelled at what you did before you got this leadership position. You have the right education and maybe you attended some specific training courses. You have gained many years of experience during

which, by trial and error, you have discovered the best way to succeed in your job.
Take some time to write the following down! Which skills you think brought you in this leadership position?

Because there are so many different jobs requiring different skills, this list will be different for everyone. Most probably however, the majority of these skills were about YOU. How YOU got your job done.

In order to meet or exceed the expectations of those who believed in you as a leader, it's important to learn what those expectations are as well. Try to discuss the motivation of those individuals who suggested you should be promoted to or hired for this particular leadership position. If that isn't possible anymore, discuss this issue with your present manager, which by the way you should do anyway.
Find out which skills they believe you possess and which skills they think are the most important for you in order to succeed in your position. Are those the same you have written down? Or are there gaps between the skills they have mentioned and your list? If so, discuss this. Find out together what is really needed and agree on that.

What do you need? Gain clarity!

Be aware that from now on, the skills that brought you here will start to become less important. The further you will travel on your leadership journey, the more important it will become how you facilitate others to get their jobs done. You will gradually move from being a specialist into being a generalist, with a major in leadership.
You need to develop additional skills and you may need help to achieve this. Discuss this as well and decide on the best

ways to go forward. Be that training, coaching on the job, coaching off the job, etc.

Endeavour to have these discussions with as many people as possible in order to obtain a multidisciplinary approach viewed from multiple angles on your position. You will discover that not everybody has the same ideas on what your leadership should look like. Get the expectations as clear as possible as soon as possible. As a leader you have to make decisions every day and when you know what is expected of you, making these decisions will become easier and the results more effective.

Unfortunately not many organisations realise you have to learn new skills. So most of the time you're on your own and you have to learn it fast – its sink or swim.

Reading books on management and leadership helps, but you also have to experiment with what you read. Put it into practice. A better way however is getting yourself trained or coached for leadership. In some cases an internal trainer or coach will help. In other cases it's better to get an external coach to help you. For both the internal- as the external coaches there are pros and cons. Either way, ask for help in your new position! Being able to ask for help is also a key skill necessary to be a good leader, you will learn this as you progress through this book.

Check on a regular basis with your manager if you're still on track with meeting his expectations.

By the way, throughout this book I use he, him and his. This is however gender unspecific. You can also read she, her and hers instead.

Is this what you've always wanted?

In the above process, you may have discovered that you're not the right person in the right place. That's perfectly alright,

it's part of the process, but what should you do now?
Two choices: adapt or leave. It sounds harsh, but that's the
way it is. Unless it's a horrible situation in which you find
yourself or it's against everything that you stand for, I would
suggest to first try to adapt.

In the beginning a lot of things you do not yet completely
understand come your way. You have to first find out what it
all means and particularly, what it means to you. You will
often feel strange and uncomfortable in certain situations.
That's what they call "out of your comfort zone" and that's
the place where you stretch your limits, where you learn. It's
the area of growth and it is huge. So your potential for
growth is huge. It's the place where you have the opportunity
to become more than you thought you could be. Suffering a
little discomfort is a small price to pay. Anyway, if you decide
to continue to grow, at a certain point you will feel
comfortable with the situation. That's an indication that you
have mastered the skills or competencies needed to do your
job.

It's then time to stretch your limits again and master new
skills and competencies. Be careful however not to be out of
your comfort zone all the time, because that may lead to
stress or a burnout. Your body and mind need periods of
comfort along your journey every now and then. You can
compare it with mountain climbers going to the top of Mount
Everest. On their way to the top they have base camps where
they can fuel up and rest before proceeding on the next leg of
their climb.

If you cannot insert comfort-stages in your work, then maybe
this is not the position you should be working in. Ask for
help and find out.

Your extended responsibilities

Remember the times that you didn't have a leadership position? Things didn't look that complicated, you were well equipped to carry out your job well. The ones leading you, in your opinion, had even more relaxed jobs and in time you wanted to become a leader as well and tell everybody what they should do while you sat back and relaxed. They would do the work for you, right?

Was it an accurate picture you had on leadership? Is it really as easy as you thought back then? Most probably you now have a different point of view. Where in the past you only had to report to your leader on your own results, you now also have to report on the results of the people you lead. Even worse, you're responsible for their results! On top of that, it might also be the case that you have to report to other stakeholders as well. You have made a step on the ladder and now more people depend on your results and on the results of those you lead. So more people are interested to know how you progress. You may be a leader now, but you're still a follower as well. A follower of your manager and your clients for instance.

You not only have to be great in motivating your team, you also have to be a great communicator. **Upward (your leaders), downward (your team), sideward (your peers) and outward (clients, suppliers and other stakeholders).** They call communication a "soft skill", but don't underestimate the power of this skill. If you master it, there's a lot you can achieve. If not, take care that you develop this skill as soon as possible. It's the number one reason why people and organisations fail!

Hard skills and soft skills

Sometimes I wonder who ever thought it was necessary to make a distinction between the two types of skills. Will you be called a hardliner if you master the hard skills? Or will you be called a softy if you're good at the soft skills? Is learning the hard skills harder than learning the soft? Some people are better at (learning) the hard skills like finance, strategic planning and such and others find it easier to practise soft skills such as communicating, listening, motivating and so on. To me it is clear that a good leader needs to be able to use both kinds of skills fluently.
It's important to be able to analyse a market and set goals to conquer that market. But when you can't motivate your team, you will probably fail to achieve those goals. It's also important to support your team and create a pleasant and harmonious working environment. But if you don't have goals to work towards, you only have a happy place with no income.
Throughout this book we will work on both the hard and soft skills, since both need to be developed in order to be a successful leader.

Overwhelmed?

You have just read through the first pages of this book. How does it feel? Feeling a bit overwhelmed already or is it your start to redefine yourself in your leadership role? Don't worry and take your time to learn and practise. You have had years of education before you started working and it took you some more years to really master the skills you now have as a professional. Don't expect to be an instant leader! Rome wasn't built in a day! You have to educate yourself again for this role.. Sure, you take the knowledge and

experience from your previous jobs with you, but the further
you develop yourself as a leader, the less you need those
skills. It's now more a question of organisational skills than
execution skills. You have to learn new skills, that's for sure.
Whether or not this is your first ever management- or
leadership book that you read or the umpteenth in an
impressive row, it is essential that you pick out the parts that
you can use in your particular situation.
*If you only read the books and don't practise what you
read, you're only developing your shelf, not yourself.*
When you practise what you read, you will actually gain
experience and find out what works and what doesn't. Not
everything I write will work in your specific situation. You
will only find out when you try. In other words "practise what
you read and practise what you need"
In the next chapter I will introduce you to the House of
Leadership. A model I have developed for you to have a
blueprint for further development of your leadership.

Dare to be vulnerable!

One of the key conditions for learning is to have an
open mind and to allow your normal pattern of thoughts to
be disrupted by the unexpected and unfamiliar. When you are
listening to someone who teaches you new things or when
you are reading a (management) book, be curious. Don't tell
yourself that you already know what they are about to say, but
continue listening or reading and ask questions. When you say
to yourself "Oh I know this", you stop listening, which means
you stop growing and you may miss important information.
Don't have an attitude that you have already reached the top
and that nobody can teach you anything new. It may surprise
you, but you will only stop learning when you're dead. The
old adage "you cannot teach an old dog new tricks" is

definitely erroneous!

With regard to the team you are leading, don't be a "Know-it-all". Consult with your team and ask for advice from them on a regular basis. They have continued being specialists and your development in that area will more than likely have slowed down, due to your need to learn a new and different set of skills that transform you from a specialist into a generalist and a great leader. Continued consultation with your team will give you new insights and will give them the recognition they deserve and appreciation for their part in the organisation. You will build stronger teams when you involve everyone in it and dare to show your vulnerability by asking for advice.

Many leaders wrongly think they have to know everything, every answer to every question. Successful leaders however do not make this mistake and they are prepared to admit they do not know everything. They leverage the knowledge and experience of many. They have strong internal and external networks and maintain those. When they receive a question they don't have the answer to, they engage their networks and harvest the correct information. It takes great managerial courage to show your vulnerability every now and then, but every great leader knows it's certainly worth it.

Victim or leader, it's up to you!

Well, by now it must be clear to you that becoming a leader is not a piece of cake. On the other hand, it's also (in most cases) not a mission impossible. There are millions of great leaders and you can become one as well. All it takes is perseverance, an open mind, some brainpower, an abundance of emotional intelligence and a sprinkling of luck and... and... and…..

But seriously, although some people are born great leaders, it doesn't mean that the rest cannot do it. With hard work and dedication, the fundamentals of a leadership mind can be learned. How about you? Do you have a leadership mind-set and are you willing to work hard? Or would you rather put your energy into surrounding yourself with people that will empathise with you and feel sorry for you and comfort you? Great leaders aren't victims! They endure hardship every once in a while, but they find ways to turn those problems into opportunities for themselves and their teams.

If you have a leadership mind-set and want to work hard, please continue with the next chapter. If you don't have that mind-set yet, but want to learn and work hard, you're also invited to continue. When you think you know it all and know what the next chapters are about – your will never be a leader.

If you prefer to stay in your role as a victim, please stop reading right here and right now. That is fine for me, I won't be offended. But be honest and go to your manager and tell him or her that you want your old job back. Maybe a real leader can then take your place. I think that's only fair.

Chapter 2 - The House of Leadership

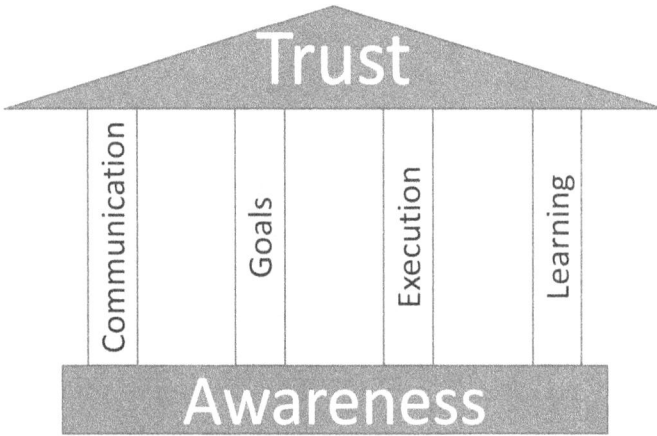

Just another model?

Welcome to your new home! I have called it "The House of Leadership". I'm glad you have chosen to continue reading. That means that you want to become a leader and you want to invest time and energy.

Is the House of Leadership just another model? YES and NO. Yes, because there is already an abundance of models, some brilliant and others totally useless (to you). And no, it's not just another model, it's my model based on fifty years of experience in life! I have developed the model based on my experience as a leader and later as a leadership trainer/ coach. Combined with a lifelong study of leadership and management I will use it through the rest of the book to

explain what you need to become a good leader, the destination of your journey. This model is your guide and shows you what to look at and which excursions you should take when you're on your journey.
It facilitates you to ask the right questions in your specific situation. It doesn't have all the answers, but it provides directions to find the answers.

Keep It Simple Stupid?

KISS! Keep It Simple Stupid!
I love this acronym. Many people have the tendency to over-complicate, thus missing the key points. If you have the skill to explain complex things in a simple way, you will find it easier to get those things done.
A good way to make complicated information easier to understand, is to use analogies or metaphors. You have just seen my metaphor, the House of Leadership, with which I want to make the complex definition of leadership easier to comprehend. With the solid foundation, I explain that you first have to understand the position you're in. Without your awareness of the situation, you cannot build the pillars carrying the roof of trust. Most answers for your leadership issues can be found by understanding the building blocks.

Start with a solid foundation: Awareness

When you are lost in a big city, you first have to find out where you are. You may use a map or have to ask others to raise your awareness.
When you have just started your journey on the way to leadership, you may also feel lost. You're in a new neighbourhood and you have to find out what everything means. You have to become aware. Aware of yourself, aware

of your environment and aware of the expectations.
Only when you have a good understanding of where you are
now and where you want to go, you will be able to find the
path you need to follow. Therefore "Awareness" is the solid
base needed to build the rest of the House of Leadership.

Build your pillars of Trust

In the Netherlands we have a saying "trust arrives by
foot and leaves on horseback", meaning that building trust
takes time and losing it can happen instantly.
As a leader you have to be trustworthy in order to build trust.
Part of it is determined by your character and other parts by
your ability to get results. The four pillars in the House of
Leaderships represent the skills you need to master, to obtain
the results to finally support the roof of trust.
You must be an excellent communicator, you must be able to
set challenging goals, you must be able to execute the plans in
order to achieve the goals and you have to be a lifelong
student.

Communication

One of the hardest soft skills to learn is
communication. It's also one of the most important skills and
very often the power of communication is underestimated.
When you have your base of awareness covered, you have to
think about what, how, when, why and with whom you have
to communicate. What are the formal communication lines?
How often do you have to be in meetings? How do you
handle your e-mail? What do you say on the telephone? How
do you solve conflicts? How do you present in front of a
group? Which communication is deliberate and what do you
say on auto pilot? Do you know the power of silence? When

should you be listening instead of talking?
A lot of questions on this subject. Be aware of your communication and ask for feedback in order to continuously improve. Make your communication a strong pillar in the House of Leadership!

Goals

Remember you were lost and that you wanted to get back to a place familiar to you? You had a goal to work to. You wanted to leave the place where you felt lost. Because you had a goal and you were aware of your situation, choosing from possibilities to get out was more effective. The same goes for organisations and in leadership. You have to have goals in order to know where to invest your energy. It will make your actions meaningful and effective. If you know how to set goals and how to execute the work to get there, you will get results and earn trust. That makes goals your second pillar to support the roof of trust.

Execution

Imagine, once more, the place in the city where you were lost. You figured out where you want to go to. In other words, your goal is clear. The next step is to make plans to get there.
Are you going to walk or find some other means of transportation? What is the very first step you have to take to get closer to your goal? Additionally, what is the next? And the next? And the next? And so on. If you put all those steps together, you have something we call a plan. Making such a plan, you already guessed, is what we define as planning. It's that simple!
The same goes for organisations. Know where you are now,

visualise where you want to go (the goal) and think about the steps to take you there (your planning). The next thing you have to do is to really take the steps (execution).

On your way towards your goal, you may find obstructions like road blocks and detours. In some cases you already had them anticipated and have a plan B, but sometimes they come as a complete surprise and you instantly have to think of a plan B. In both cases the focus must be on the goal and your solution must be towards reaching that goal. When you are travelling towards your goals you must also use your skills and knowledge, your leadership compass, to regularly check where you are. Are you still heading towards your goal or are you moving away from it? If the latter is the case, what do you need to do to get back on track?

Learning

Of course, you can learn as you go. Live by the seat of your pants and be surprised every time things turn out different than you thought and improvise and devise solutions at the moment that things go pear-shaped! . Another, and maybe better, approach is that you first take some time to prepare yourself by learning what you need to know, as the old saying goes "a stitch in time saves nine". This will help you to avoid most of the surprises and to expect the unexpected. In the analogy of getting lost in the city, study the map of the city before you go, get information on (public) transport, know how to recognise certain landmarks, etc.

In the real world you will have a combination of both approaches. Sometimes you learn on the job -flying by the seat of your pants- and in some cases you have the opportunity to proactively educate yourself - a stitch in time saves nine. For instance by training or coaching or by reading management books. When you continue to learn, you continue to grow.

All under the roof of Trust

I am a huge fan of Stephen R. Covey and read his material on a regular basis. Every time I learn something new and I then apply that to my life and business. When I see it works, that builds trust. It makes me trust myself as well as the wisdom of Stephen R. Covey. Unfortunately he is not alive anymore, but his legacy lives on.
His son Stephen M.R. Covey co-wrote a book with Rebecca R. Merrill, called "The Speed of Trust". This is a book I urge you to read (of course after this one), because it will show you how to build trust and what trust really means in terms of time and money. It shows different levels of trust (personal, relational, organisational, in the market and in society) and also what determines trust. To me it's absolutely without doubt that good leadership can only be sustained under a roof of trust.
If you, in your organisation, find that trust is lacking or non-existent, find ways to restore it. Don't think in terms of quick fixes, but do it thoroughly. If necessary, build a new roof!

Adaptive design

All organisations are different. Some are big, some small, some are very hierarchical others flat, some are production oriented, others people oriented, some are profit orientated and some are non-profit orientated and so on and so forth. Some principles however apply to all organisations. It is up to you to find out how they fit into your specific situation and your specific organisation or even team. With the House of Leadership I provide you with a model that you

can stretch or shrink to your situation. You have to build and
decorate it yourself.
The same principles apply to the different levels, only the
magnitude changes.

Know the neighbourhood

When you build or buy a house, you also want to
know what the neighbourhood is like. The same goes for the
House of Leadership. You want to know what is going on
around your House of Leadership. Which forces (positive and
negative) are working for or against it? What do you need to
do to keep your house strong and ensure that the forces are
balanced in favour of the positive effects? Is there a hurricane
on its way? Is there a termite infestation? Do you need to
reinforce certain parts or carry out special conservation
treatments? What should you do to withstand storms? Where
can you benefit from outside circumstances? In the
management world it is often looked at as a SWOT analysis.
What are the "Strengths" and "Weaknesses" of your house –
internal- and what are the "Opportunities" and "Threats"
outside your house – external? Recognising and
understanding these forces, will help you make better
decisions, strategically and operationally.

Maintenance

Once you have a solid house, you want to keep it
solid. In line with the previous paragraph, you have to
regularly survey your house. Are the strengths still as strong
as they were? Have you improved on your weaknesses?
Which new weaknesses are visible and are the foundations
still strong enough to hold your house and prevent
subsidence?

Not only do you have to make an assessment of your house, you also have to continuously scan your neighbourhood. Are the opportunities and threats still there? Are they as strong as they were? Do they still influence your leadership, team or organisation?

Since your strengths, weaknesses, opportunities and threats continually change, you have to maintain your House of Leadership and adapt to these changes. Some markets show bigger and more frequent changes than others and that means that, when you're in those markets, you have to carry out more maintenance in order to keep adapting.

Sometimes you have to work on your foundation of awareness (reality check) and sometimes you have some re-work on one of the pillars or you may find that the roof of trust is leaking and needs repair.

In short, work on your House of Leadership is never finished.

Chapter 3 - Lines? What lines?

A simple exercise

Please have a look at the picture below and take a piece of paper to draw that same picture yourself.

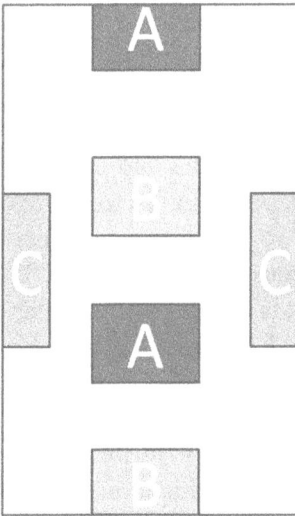

When you have drawn the picture, draw lines from A to A, B to B and C to C, without letting the lines cross each other. For people familiar with technical line drawings, also not with a jump over bridge. All three lines must be drawn at the front side of the paper, just two-dimensional. The paper just lies flat on a table or desk. No folding or other tricks, just a plain exercise where you draw three non-crossing lines on a piece of paper.
When you don't succeed immediately, try harder, but don't

worry, it has nothing to do with your intelligence. It's more about your ability to act and finish what you have started. The solution for this exercise and the reason why I have asked you to solve this problem can be found on the website: http://www.leadbetweenthelines.com/simple-exercise/

Why lines?

Why did I call my book "Lead Between the Lines"? Originally because I wanted to write about leadership in an industrial environment, between oil filled pipe lines. Within such an environment, you also have to deal with many contacts. Here I visualised the many communication lines between the leader and all these contacts. Further, within an industrial environment you will find many rules and procedures. I pictured these as lines on paper or in electronic documents. Although you have to stick to the rules, you sometimes also have to read between the lines to find solutions. This finally brought me to the title of this book, Lead Between the Lines. I found out however, that what I am writing about is not only applicable to industrial environments. It can be used in all kinds of organisations. It is universal.

Now I see "Lead Between the Lines" more as picturing your place within your organisation. Within a hierarchy or a network. Where you're not only a leader, but also a follower and a peer. It's about how you lead, follow and influence. How do you communicate on the various levels? How do you wear many different hats at the same time? What are the differences when you communicate on the work floor or when you communicate in the board room? Which lines do you follow and which do you cross?

Be aware that not all lines are straight(forward). For example an organisation will usually have formal and informal leaders!

Organisations

In order to make clear who reports to whom, organisations use organisation charts. Within these charts, you can see the various levels in an organisation. Depending on the size of the organisation, one chart can describe the whole organisation or just one department. Typically you will find the highest in command on top of the chart and going down in the organisation, the chart broadens. Below you will see a typical organisation chart that has been in use for decades now.

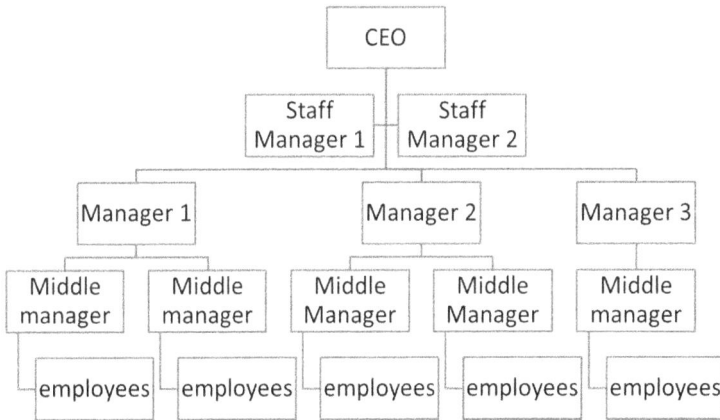

Nowadays you will find more variations, because companies also want to organise differently. Or at least they want to give the impression that they do. The hierarchical chart has proven its use during the last century and is continuing to do so. However, nowadays far more information is readily available and a growing group of professionals doesn't want to be led that way anymore. Now you will see an increasing shift from the traditional hierarchical chart towards networking models. From formal to informal.

Referring to the hierarchical model, closer to the top the focus is on strategy and when you're going to the levels below, operations become increasingly important. One of your roles as a leader is to bring those two aspects - strategy and operations- into equilibrium.

Networks

We have arrived in the information age and organisations are not at all as simple as projected in the traditional organisation charts. There are many more lines active than can be drawn in these charts. The formal lines are greatly outnumbered by the informal ones. So, as a leader, you must not only be aware of all those lines acting within and outside your organisation, but you also have to be active within these networks.
This requires a great flexibility from leaders, but also a very high focus on the goals. It is easy to be very busy in the wrong networks and thus steering away from reaching your goals. If you lose focus, achieving results will be very hard. Get a reality check every now and then and find out which networks help you, your team and your organisation.

Lines of command

Who is giving the orders? Who is the boss? To whom do you need to report? Most larger organisations have these kind of questions well defined in quality systems with procedures, flowcharts and functional descriptions and so on. In smaller, often more flexible, organisations these lines are less clear and sometimes non-existent..
In the end it's the market that is "giving the orders" to the organisations and it is from there that organisations should be defined.

In the beginning all those lines will be confusing, but make sure you will find out how these lines run within your environment and what that means for you as a leader. Be careful with your communication. Many leaders don't like it very much when they are bypassed.

Communication lines

Not all communication is going through the lines of command. Or more accurately said, most communication is going on outside those lines! There are many grapevines, coffee machines and smoking corners where employees discuss issues at work (and much more).
Should you try to be everywhere in order to hear what they all have to say (about you)? No, don't even try! Just be aware that these conversations take place. The more you're trying to control them, the less you will hear and the more they will be talking behind your back. Better to direct your energy at creating an open culture, where people feel free to speak up. Take a look at your organisation. Which lines of communication do you see? Formal or informal, internal or external, written or spoken, verbal or non-verbal? The better you understand the lines of communication, the better you can use them to reach your goals.

Direct or indirect

How do you communicate? Do you say things as they are, directly to the person it concerns? Or do you use a more indirect approach? Do you make use of others to influence the person it concerns or to convey your message? Different cultures have different habits and rules when it comes to communication. Sometimes you must be an expert in reading between the lines to understand the deeper meaning of some messages.

Some countries prefer an indirect approach over a direct one, but also different groups have different cultures and different ways of communication. In the eyes of the Chinese for instance, the Dutch are painfully direct, whereas the Dutch think the Chinese are beating around the bush. If you recognize these differences and respect them, you will optimise your conversations and increase the likelihood of reaching your goals.

Especially in multicultural and multinational organisations it's a huge advantage if you are aware of cultural differences and adapt your style.

Crossing the line

Sometimes it's better to say sorry than to ask for permission. As a leader, you have to take (calculated) risks every now and then. This may also mean that you are crossing someone's line. I say "someone's line" on purpose, because everybody has a different threshold when it comes to line crossing.

For you it is good to understand where your most important stakeholders (people you lead, people who lead you, customers, suppliers, etc.) have drawn their lines. It helps you to determine which decisions may bring trouble and how big your sorry should be when you have actually crossed that line. Crossing lines occasionally is good for your development as a leader, but crossing lines too often or too far can also be harmful to your career and for the cohesion of your team. So, be careful, but not afraid!

The House of Leadership

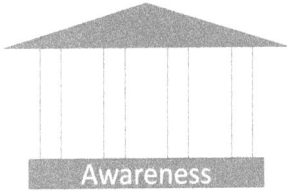

What we have discussed in this chapter has mostly to do with you gaining awareness of where you stand in your organisation and what goes on around you.

My aim with all the chapters is that you think about what is going on around you and how you manage the tsunami of information in order to lead successfully.

Now you know more about what's going *around* you, you need to learn more about yourself and how you lead yourself. That's the topic of the next chapter.

Chapter 4 - Who am I anyway?

Lead yourself before you lead others

Can you lead others if you cannot even lead yourself? Have you ever thought about this question? Have you got a mind-set for leadership or do they need to tell you exactly what to do? If you can't lead yourself, don't expect that you can lead others.

In leading yourself you have to possess, or develop, a few skills. You have to get a clear focus on where you want to go, a mission. What do you want to achieve? How do you see yourself in, say, five to ten years from now? What is your vision?

Furthermore, you must have the discipline to continuously work towards your goals. That means that you have to prioritise your actions. Go through your to-do list every day in order to plan ahead those items that are really important. Don't let yourself be distracted by time wasters.

In order to be able to lead yourself, you also need to be proactive. Don't wait until someone asks you to do something, but anticipate. Be aware of what has to be done and get yourself into gear. Proactive is the opposite of reactive. Reactive people's actions depend on the circumstances. When the weather is bad, their mood is bad. When the weather is bright, their mood is bright.

For proactive people these circumstances are not that important. They act on what is important, no matter what. They take the time to think things over before they respond.

Discover who you are

Apart from knowing where you want to be in ten years from now, you also need to know what kind of person you are. What is your character like? What are your bright sides, but also what are your dark sides? What kind of person would you like to be. What would you like people to say about you when you're not with them?

Take a piece of paper and write down which personal traits make you proud and which make you a little less happy. Take your time for this exercise and write down as much about yourself as possible. Think about situations in your family, at home, at work, with friends, at your sports club, when you're doing charity work, etc. What gives you energy? What are energy drainers? Who or what are the atmosphere hoovers in your life?

The next step is to use this information to construct your own personal mission statement. Who are you, what do you stand for, what do you want to contribute in your life and what do you want to achieve? Make it a real statement in a positive and present tense, starting with: "I, your name....."

A personal mission statement will help you decide what to do when you have many options at hand. It helps you making the right decisions to achieve what you have promised yourself. Not many people go to the trouble of writing their own personal mission statement, but all <u>successful</u> people do! Write down your first draft now and refine it during your progress through the chapters of this book. In these chapters you will learn more about yourself and that will help you improve your statement.

Maybe my personal mission statement will help you:

"I, Sjoerd de Waal, am trustworthy and a person of high integrity, with a good sense of humour.
I consider it important and enjoyable to develop myself, other people and organisations.
My family, friends and clients can count on my sincerity, love and warmth. I am open to criticism and use that for my development."

What are you good at?

By now you have more insights of who you are, who you want to be, where you want to go and which traits make you feel good or not so good. You have a vision of where you want to be in about ten years. Is it a bold one or did you stay on the safe side? Did you dare to step out of your comfort zone? Look at your mission statement again and make it five times more challenging! Don't be too modest! You only have one life, make it worth living! What do you need to accomplish what you have envisioned? Which skills, what attitude and which other resources?
In the last paragraph you have made a list of your personal traits and also what energises you or drains your energy. Which of those energising and well developed traits can you use to fulfil your mission?
Later in this chapter, I will offer you a solution that you can use to get a detailed insight in your preferred way of thinking.

Your personal SWOT

In business, a SWOT (Strengths, Weaknesses, Opportunities, Threats) is a frequently used instrument to analyse the company and market. From this analysis an organisation can make plans to serve a market in a profitable way. The strengths and weaknesses are part of the internal analysis and the opportunities and threats concern the external analysis.

Why not use a SWOT to analyse yourself? What have you got that helps or hinders you to achieve your goals? And what external factors may help or hinder your aspirations? You have already gone through your internal analysis in the previous paragraphs, so let's now shift to your environment. Take a good look around you for both opportunities and threats. Look in your private life (family, friends), your professional life (what is going on in your organisation?) and society in general (what trends are visible, what new technology is available, what happens socially and culturally?). Once you have found all strengths, weaknesses, opportunities and threats, you can have a look at how well you're equipped to profit from opportunities and withstand threats.

This you can do with a SWOT confrontation matrix (see the template). You can make one in Excel or just draw one with pen and paper or on a flip-over board. For your first draft, I would suggest the latter and use the space available.

	O1:	O2:	O3:	O4:	O5:	T1:	T2:	T3:	T4:	T5:	
					Opportunities:				Threats:		
Strengths:											Pluses
S1:			+	++							3
S2:		++				++	++				6
S3:						+	++				3
S4:								++			2
S5:									++		2
Weaknesses:											Minuses
W1:	--										2
W2:			-				--	--	--		7
W3:		--							-		3
W4:				-			--		-		4
W5:			--								2
Pluses		2	1	2		3	4	2	2		
Minuses	2	2	3	1			4	2	4		

Fill in your top five Strengths, Weaknesses, Opportunities and Threats. Which Strengths can you leverage to profit from the Opportunities? Which Weaknesses hinder you to profit from these? Which Strengths help you overcome Threats and which Weaknesses put you in real danger when they're confronted with the Threats? Use a scale from -- to ++ to indicate the impact.
When you have your confrontation matrix ready, let others look at it as well and let them fill in the blanks.

Where should you involve others?

You may know now which traits will help you to realise your mission. On the other side, you may have found there are also some traits missing or underdeveloped. Maybe they drain your energy, but you know you need them to get further on your way. Time to call in the cavalry!
For some skills or traits you may need others to coach or train you. For the other skills or traits you may need people to whom you can delegate or outsource activities. Evaluate critically what you really need and how you involve others.

Blind spots (ask others)

Why did I suggest you would ask others to fill in your blanks? Because everybody has got blind spots. Things, skills or habits you aren't aware of, but that are visible to others. If you know people with whom you share a high level of trust, ask them for honest feedback and to help you find your blind spots. Look at your confrontation matrix, but also ask for general feedback with respect to your blind spots. They may point out some additional opportunities and threats you weren't aware of – this is a bonus.

Pictures or bullet points?

You have probably heard this before, the vast majority of humans have right and a left side brains. Oh what a shock, they work differently. It's just something we take for granted most of the time, but being aware of this fact and using it to your advantage in the way you lead, will help you achieve more.

Nowadays technology helps neuroscientists around the world discover interesting new things about how our brains function. Many of these discoveries are very helpful for people working together.

You may, for instance, like to immerse yourself deeply in the subject matter and focus on the fine details. You may like structure and analysis before you make decisions. You use bullet points and text to make your point. These are some of the characteristics of left brain thinkers. On the other hand other people prefer to look at the big picture, make decisions based on their gut feelings and use pictures and stories to make their point. If you are not aware of these two sorts of thinkers and cannot distinguish between the two, you may have trouble understanding each other.

Knowing how your brain is wired up and also knowing that it is different for everyone, will help you make better decisions, helps you communicate more effectively and make you a better leader, getting better results.

This is why I have "awareness" as the foundation of the House of Leadership.

Brain preferences

When you know what your preferred way of thinking is, you will be more effective in your leadership. There are some tools available that will help you discover more about yourself. Some are useless, but others are very good and scientifically proven.

Take, for instance, the Neethling Brain Instruments, developed by Dr. Kobus Neethling. He started his extensive neuro-scientific research in the 80's and has, over time, developed a scientifically proven system. This system will help you discover yourself in terms of your preferred way of thinking.

The NBI method has specific questionnaires for specific situations. The NBI General Adult Assessment, the basis, consists of two questionnaires, one giving you insight which brain preferences come naturally to you. It gives you insight in which cluster of brain preferences you score higher and in which you score lower. NBI divides these preferences in four quadrants and eight dimensions. Each person has a unique profile by scoring lesser or higher in each quadrant and dimension.

The information you will get out of your assessment will help you a great deal. In your personal life, as a professional, in your leadership, with your communication, your career path, your relations, etc. etc.

I am an NBI-licencee and as such, I can carry out the NBI General Adult Assessment at a highly reduced price. This is the offer I referred to earlier!

Just go to www.leadbetweenthelines.com/bonuses and use login code **LBTL2014** to enter this private page. You will find a very interesting offer for the assessment plus three additional FREE bonuses.

If you're interested in learning more about assessing brain preferences of others, there are training programs to become a licencee, just like I am. You will learn how to interpret behaviours and situations so that you can adapt your communication and behaviour. If you want to know if you, as a leader, or your company is doing well in the eyes of the employees, you can also decide to roll out the Employee

Engagement Scan.

For more information on other NBI® products or training,
please contact me at book@leadbetweenthelines.com.

Whole brain or no brain?

Unfortunately there are many managers who think
that when you hold a certain position, you must be good in all
aspects of that position. In the annual performance reviews
they focus on areas that need further development. Most of
the time it's in areas you're not good at or have no affinity
with or have no talent for. Instead of looking for colleagues
that love to take over those aspects, because they have
different brain preferences, you will be send to a training or
you get a deadline to improve yourself. Result: two de-
motivators! You have to learn things you don't want to and
your colleague doesn't get the opportunity to help you with
work he or she loves to do.

Not all people hate to work with numbers and not all people
panic in a seemingly chaotic environment.

It is no brain when you try to teach a fish how to run and it's
whole brain when you design the work to be done around the
talents of your employees.

Talk with the group and find out who loves to execute which
tasks. There may be some tasks nobody likes. Find out if they
are necessary and if yes, distribute them evenly. They will
understand, because you have done your best to let people do
what they like best.

The House of Leadership

In this chapter we have focused on you. Who are you as a person and as a leader? What are your strengths and weaknesses? How can you profit from opportunities and steer clear from threats?
We also addressed the fact that all people have different brain preferences and that these brain preferences determine how you communicate, lead and work in teams.

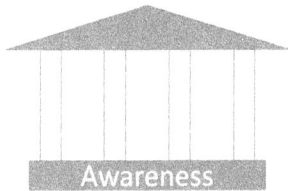

Combining the strengths of people with different brain preferences will help you build a collaborative group.
Focusing on weaknesses on the other hand leads to a no brain group.

All of the subjects we have discussed fall in the foundation of the House of Leadership, "Awareness". Awareness of yourself and a little bit awareness of your team.

In the next chapter we will go a step further and look at other actors in your environment.

Don't forget to go to www.leadbetweenthelines.com/bonuses to claim your free bonuses and order the assessment at the reduced price. Use login code LBTL2014 to enter the page. The bonuses and special offer are exclusively for my readers.

Chapter 5 - Am I on my own?

Who cares?

To start with answering the chapter's question: no, you're not on your own. When you are a leader, you lead at least one other person. But most probably you lead more, maybe a small team or a project or even a complete organisation.

Question number two: who cares? You might be surprised! A lot of people are influenced by what you are doing, so many people actually care.

Take a few minutes to think this over: What is your supply chain? Who are delivering services or products to you? To whom are you supplying and what? Make a list of all people, departments and organisations you can think of.

Take your team for instance. They depend upon your leadership. Do you provide them with the right resources to be successful? Are you actually supporting their development? Is it a team or a collection of individuals? How are the relationships with the managers at the same hierarchical level as you? Do you help each other or are you internal competitors? How do your top managers divide the resources?

Who else in your personal supply chain can you think of?

Networks

Look at yourself as a spider in a web. In the previous paragraph we have satisfied the left brainers with a list of people, departments and organisations that cared about you.

Now let's connect to the right brainers too and make a
network graphic with badges and connection lines.
Put yourself in the centre and place the listed people,
departments and organisations around you. How are they
connected to you and how are they connected to each other?
Below you will find what such a diagram could look like. For
your exercise, I suggest that you take a flip-over chart and
play around with all the connections. Maybe it's a good idea
to start with using Post-it® Notes for all the connections.
They can easily be repositioned. Unfortunately, that is what
some managers think about people too...

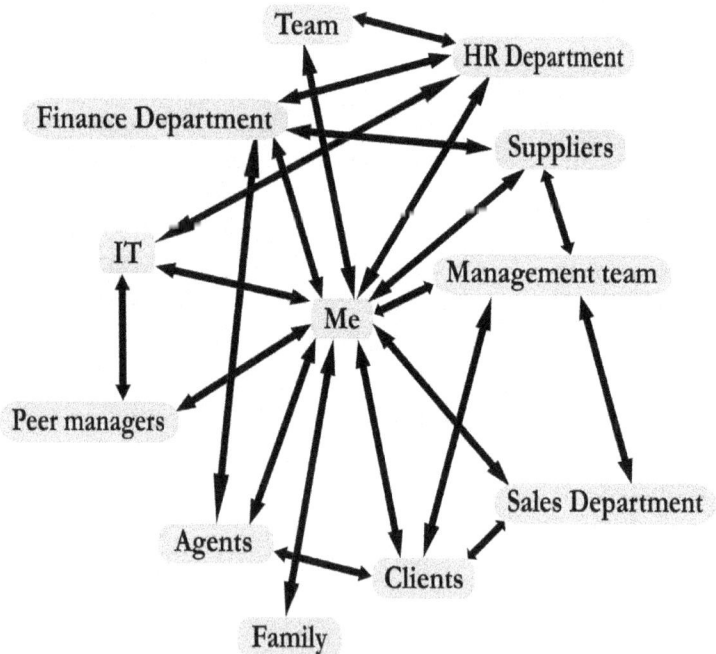

Online, offline or both?

In today's information age, being connected isn't a choice anymore. It's mandatory. With an enormous choice of different social media channels, it can be hard to choose the right ones. Some of them come and go, some are only used in certain countries and others never grow big enough to make an impact. From a professional point of view, the one network you should be connected to is LinkedIn. Many members just use it as a giant resume depository, but there is much more to it. You can find out a lot of information about people, organisations, situations and technologies that are important to you or your organisation. When used cleverly, it's also a great marketing tool. When you participate in group discussions, you can turn the spotlight on your company or yourself and make interesting new connections. If you want to connect to a certain person within a certain company, use the search options and see to whom in your own network the person you're looking for is connected. Maybe he can introduce you.

Other useful networks are Facebook (pages), Google+, YouTube and Twitter. I have said it before, there are many more, but assessing those is beyond the scope of this book. Online networking is great, but it can never totally replace the face-to-face variant. Meet and greet your contacts frequently and keep the connection interesting for them.

Some people have trouble understanding the online technology and others fear talking to strangers or keeping a good relationship. For the first category: Get help! For the second category: Get help! To benefit from a good network, it's important that you feel at ease with both variants, online and offline.

Internal networking

Have you already experienced how much harder it is to sell internally than it is to sell to a customer? Trying to get support for your ideas, getting another department to deliver its promises or getting additional manpower for your department. Internal selling is an important skill if you want to get to results.

Therefore it's obvious that you need to invest time and energy in maintaining your internal network. Stay in touch with your peer managers, your upper management and your own team. Listen to their challenges and be cooperative where you can. Your internal networking must grease the internal activities of the organisation.

Depending on your functional power only seldom generates the same or better results. Being helpful to others doesn't mean you have to be weak. You don't have to say "yes" to everything. Reserve that answer for important matters only, matters that help the organisation move closer towards its goals.

External networking

For some leadership positions within an organisation you have to do a lot of external networking and for others an external network is virtually non-existent. It doesn't matter too much if you have a large or a small external network, in both cases you have to maintain it properly.

First have a look who is populating your external network. Are they suppliers, clients, officials, competitors or people living in the vicinity of your company? All these contacts have their own specific needs and have to be treated in a way fitting those needs. A small negligence may end up in a huge problem, so knowing your network is crucial.

Be aware of the power of social media. A poisonous tweet or message on Facebook can do a lot of harm before you even realise what happened.

In addition, keep a keen eye on the external contacts your team members have. Remember, you are responsible for their actions and results as well. What is the level of trust within your team? A typical rule of thumb: if you treat your team well and you're available to them, they will usually treat their (external) contacts well too.

The key to networking

How can I help you? That's the key to networking! By helping others and not expecting something in return, you build the strongest networks. If you share, you will find that favours will be returned. Sometimes by those you've helped, sometimes by others. Be willing to give and be willing to receive.

The ways in which you can help others are infinite, but I will give you some examples to help you on your way. Share knowledge, refer customers to suppliers you have good experiences with, share market information, work together in projects, etc.

When you meet new people, listen to their story first and find areas where you can connect. Don't try to push your products or services through their throats. Take your time to build a relationship and find out what they really need, build trust. When time comes and you have the products or services satisfying their needs, they will come to you.

Influence

Too often influencing people is confused with manipulating them. There is however a distinct difference.

When you're influencing people, you go for a situation where at least they and maybe you benefit (win-win).
When you're manipulating, it's all about you. If they also benefit, they're lucky, but it's not your primary objective. Consciously or unconsciously, we're all influencing (and sometimes manipulating) others. And the other way around, them influencing us, also happens frequently.
In your thinking you're influenced by a lot of things. It can be by experiences from the past, your mood, the circumstances you're in, your physical situation, your psychological situation, etc. This will also influence your decision-making. If you are aware of this and dare to question your observations, you will collect more and better information and enhance your decision-making.
Who do you influence? Is that positive or negative? Does it help those persons in their development?
By whom or what are you influenced? Does it help you? Can you share it with others?
Good influencers are inspirational and add value for others. Be aware of your role as a leader. People are modelling you, so you are a role model. Is the behaviour they are modelling positive? If not, do a reality check and investigate your own behaviour.

Your team

In chapter one I wrote that, as a leader, you have extended responsibilities. Not only your own results count, but also those of your team. In the last paragraph I showed you that you are a role model and that you have an influence on the team results. Your team is more or less your mirror. So if you want to have a perfect team, start working on a perfect you first. Be a positive example and network within your team. What can you do for them, so that they can perform at their peaks? What are their brain preferences? What are their talents? Do you judge them on their talents or on their flaws? How do you help them improving on themselves? Is what they are doing really what they like to do or do they feel pushed by you?

Maintain your team well and results will follow. Do you need help? Get help! From inside or outside, but don't neglect your team. It's the extended you and negligence will backfire on you.

The House of Leadership

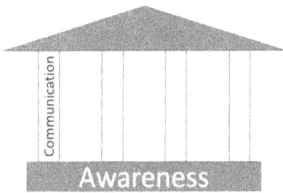

In this chapter we have made your foundation of awareness stronger again by identifying your stakeholders. You've gained more insight in your internal and external networks and found what is important when you are networking. The core to networking is: "How can I help you?"

We have scratched the surface on the pillar of communication, one of the most important skills in the House of Leadership. How do you communicate within your networks? How does your communication and behaviour translate in results?

In the next chapter we will continue with the pillars of communication and goals. But we will also add more strength to your foundation of awareness.

On my webpage www.leadbetweenthelines.com/bonuses, I have uploaded a free video for you in which I explain the House of Leadership.

Feel free to download the free bonuses, using code LBTL2014 to enter the page.

Chapter 6 - What do they want from me?

Stakeholders

We have seen it in the last chapter, you're not on your own and actually there is a wealth of people connected to you and your organisation. All those people influenced by your work, in whatever way, are the so-called stakeholders. However, they don't all share the same level of interest or power. It varies from person to person and therefore, the effort you have to put into the communication with them varies as well. Now let's go back to your list or graphic of those people you have identified to care about you and your activities. How much effort do you think you have to put in for each of them?

Map and discover

In order to find out how much effort you should put into the relationships with your stakeholders, you can map their influence. The easiest and clearest way is to make a matrix. I suggest to make one on a flip-over chart, so that you have enough space to map them all. On the horizontal axis you make a scale ranging from low to high interest and on the vertical one from low to high power. If it gives you more insight, you can also add a scale from 1 to 5 to both axes. Now take your list or graphic from the last chapter and plot those names in the matrix, based on their power and interest concerning you and your activities. Put in the names of people, not departments or companies. You deal with people. When you have filled your quadrants, you have four different groups, each of which has to be treated differently. In general, these are your groups:

1 . **High power - high interest:** involve them completely and do your utmost to keep them satisfied
2 . **High power - low interest:** invest just enough time and trouble to keep them satisfied, but beware not to bore them with your communication.
3 . **Low power - high interest:** keep them well informed and talk to them regularly. They may be useful to you and in time they may also gain power.
4 . **Low power - low interest:** just know they are there, but don't bother them with an overload of information.

Use your matrix for further reference in your work. It is also very useful to further analyse the importance and specifics of your major stakeholders.

Who wants what?

Now that you know who has power and who is interested, it's time for the next step. What exactly are they interested in? Two people in the quadrant high power - high interest can have totally opposite interests. Your direct manager probably has different interests then your contact at your key supplier. Your manager may want to cut costs, whereas the key supplier wants to sell more to you. Both can have a high power and high interest.
Make it a priority to find out what is important for who. Decide on the contents and frequency of your communication with at least your high power stakeholders. Make appointments with your high power - high interest stakeholders to discuss what kind of information they want from you, how often and through which channels. Find out

their impression about your work. Are they positive, neutral or negative towards you or your team? What do you need to do to transform their negative feelings into positive experiences? Your invitation to discuss your relationship with them is already a very big first step.

Friend or foe?

Not all stakeholders will be happy with your successes, so not everyone will be as supportive as you would like. That your competitors will be less happy with your successes is clear. Some organisations foster internal competition and that means that you will find your competitors externally as well as internally. If your organisation has a culture of internal competition, identify your competitors and invite them for meetings to change the culture into one of collaboration towards organisational goals. Most of the time, internal competition is fiercer than external competition and it lowers the company's external competitive power.
Identifying the positives, neutrals and negatives helps you to consciously make your plans successful. There are simply too many stakeholders to keep track of in an unstructured way. If you put effort in maintaining the relationships, you can get help from your friends and keep the foes calm.

Areas of conflict

Some managers always try to avoid conflict and others actively seek it. Effective leaders know how and when to avoid it or when they should go into a conflict situation in order to find solutions.
Conflicts have a negative reputation, but they can also be very useful. When you're open to learn, you can profit from them.

Try to understand the different points of view from the parties and search for solutions where all can benefit. I know it takes courage, but it pays off.

In his book "The seven habits of highly effective leaders", Dr. Stephen Covey identified three habits to grow from independence to interdependence. These habits are:

- Habit 4: Think win-win
- Habit 5: Seek first to understand, then to be understood
- Habit 6: Synergize

Making these habits your habits, will hugely increase your ability to handle conflicts and turn them into opportunities for the parties involved. I highly recommend you to read this bible for leaders. To me (and many others) it was life- and career-changing.

Mission, vision and values

In chapter 4, I've asked you to write down your own personal mission statement. It should describe you, your values and what you want to contribute in life.

Organisations also have missions and visions. Unfortunately many have been designed by a select group within the organisation and are only there to make a good impression on the outside world. Many are skilfully crafted sentences that are hard to learn by heart and certainly don't resonate with the people who should support them, the employees.

Effective mission statements are SHARED mission statements. Not broadcast to the world, but jointly developed with the people working within the organisation.

Yeah, sure, but how about large corporations with corporate communication departments taking care of it? Well, if it is a competent corporate communication department, they already have involved people from all levels throughout the company. If not, you make a start for your department. Take the corporate mission statement, discuss the meaning of it with your team and find a way to make a shared mission statement for your team, supporting the corporate mission statement. Watch what it does to your team.

Hierarchy of goals

How well is your mission statement aligned with that of the organisation? And how about your goals? In my career I have talked to many people in leadership positions and most of them could not tell me what the mission and vision of their company is. They only had a minimal knowledge of the goals their companies tried to achieve.
For many managers goal setting is just one of those things you do at the end of a year and it is not in their list of favourites. They think they already have enough on their mind and setting goals consumes too much time, a resource they never have enough of.
This way of thinking mostly results in taking last year's goals and add some new goals to it. In case of financial goals some small percentages are added or subtracted here and there. It will be no surprise to you that these methods are not what you call sustainable.
In difficult times or markets, these companies soon will cease to exist. A better way of goal setting is by looking at the overall company goals and set up supporting goals for each layer and department within the company. These deduced goals together should make the company goals attainable.
For you, your department's goals help you to decide where the team's focus should be on, and to discuss the individual goals of your team members.

The House of Leadership

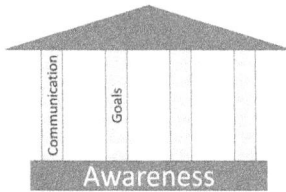

Another chapter reaching its end. Again we have carried out a lot of work on the foundation of awareness. By now you must have a far better view of your current position.

You have mapped your most important stakeholders and you have a better knowledge of what they expect from you and what you can expect from them. This is knowledge you have gained by communicating with them. Now that you have a better overview, you also understand their (re)actions and responses better. This will help you to decide if you need to enter into extensive discussions or not.

Although they have a negative annotation, conflicts can be very healthy and, when handled well, enhance growth.

So, we have worked on the pillar of communication and also on the pillar of goals. This is where we will continue with in the next chapter as well, when we look at what you want from them.

Don't forget to go to www.leadbetweenthelines.com/bonuses. I have some free bonuses on goal setting and goal getting. In addition I have some free bonuses on the House of Leadership waiting for you to pick them up. Use LBTL2014 as your login code to enter the page.

Chapter 7 - What do I want from them?

Top down, bottom up

Who is setting the goals? And how do we motivate everyone to achieve those goals? Traditionally, goal setting was done top down. A few wise men at the top decided what to do the coming year and the large group below them was expected to execute what was necessary to achieve these goals.

Although this method still has many practitioners, it's not the optimum. Just as with the mission statement, vision and values, goals should be shared goals. If the top of the organisation ignores the experience, knowledge, creativity and wisdom of the crowd, the least that will happen is that they miss out on great opportunities.

So if you are part of a management team, organise strategic sessions. Let the members of the large group below the top contribute with their visions and ideas. You will be surprised by the innovative power of the group.

An additional advantage of inviting those who are interested in contributing, is that they will do far more to actually achieve the goals. After all, they were part of the construction team. They are engaged.

When you are a lower level leader, you can do the same with the group you lead. When you start changing the habits and people see you're successful, more managers will follow your example.

Aligning goals

When goal setting is done correctly, all departments' and individual goals added up should result in the company's goals being achieved.
After the top has used the critical mass of the group to develop a set of goals, the company's goals have to be cascaded down. Through the business units, departments, teams, all the way down to every individual employee, leaders and managers included. Each will get its own set of goals, ultimately contributing to the company's goals.
When you have aligned the goals this way, be aware that other departments, teams and individuals are working towards the same goals and that you have to collaborate with them. It's then important to share the time frames and identify common critical steps and the rate determining steps, especially when there are interdependent activities. This way you work effectively and efficiently towards the same goals. Sometimes, even within the same company, there are conflicting goals for different entities within an organisation. For instance Finance needs to bring the overall costs down, whereas Research & Development has to invest in new technologies to stay up to date. If you have to deal with conflicting goals, discuss them and get clarity for all parties involved. After having gained clarity, find alternatives to improve on the existing set of goals. For this, you can use creative thinking techniques.

Use your team when making plans

Do you still believe you should be the only one defining the lines for your team? The only one telling your team what to do and how to do it? Or are you convinced now that you should use the power of synergy within your team?

Be aware that, now you're a leader, you're not the specialist anymore. You may still have a lot of knowledge with regard to your former specialism, but you have to develop yourself in a different direction now. Use the experience, skills and intelligence of the group and they will reward you with their increased motivation to get to results. Involving your team members in goal setting and planning will increase their level of engagement. They are part of the plans right from the start and that makes them own the plans. You don't need to apply a lot of pressure anymore to get things done.

Are you struggling with a project right now or do you have to make plans for a new project? Get your people involved and see what happens.

Test the plans

When you want to translate the goals into strategic planning, you need ideas. As mentioned in the last paragraph, you should involve your team in this stage. A good way to do that is by creative thinking, preferably with the use of a facilitator (internal or external).

Not all ideas are good. In fact, most of them are not that good at all. But that does not mean that they should be withheld. When you participate in a creative thinking session, you need to bring up as many ideas as possible, without judging them right away.

Why? Because the chances are better to find one good idea when you have many and also, what starts as a bad idea may trigger other ideas that prove to be good ones. If you have gone through the brainstorming phase, it is time to judge. With the group you determine the top 5 to 10 ideas that are worth further investigation. From these 5 to 10 ideas, you make a further reduction to maybe three. You judge them by checking whether they can be executed within a fair period or not and if the idea is average or innovative. In other words: does it have a wow! in it?

If they can be executed and they are good, you have to make plans to actually implement them. And of course you have to test your plans before you start with the execution.

Questions you have to answer are:

- Is your plan concrete?
- Do the steps make sense?
- Have you identified pitfalls and obstacles?
- Who else will benefit?
- How certain can you be about the outcome?
- Do you have the resources? Can they be obtained?

Be critical and take your time to find the right answers. If you don't have the time to do it well the first time, you certainly won't have time to redo it after you have failed in the execution stage.

Fuzzy or SMART?

Is it absolutely clear now to everyone involved? Is it a clear plan with clear responsibilities and accountabilities? Is the time frame clear and do you have the resources?

Or is it more like "let's just start and we'll see where it ends"? For smaller routine tasks, with minor consequences, such a fuzzy start can be perfectly alright. In most cases however and certainly for annual goals, it's better to have a good structure. SMART goal setting is a widely used structure and stands for:

- **S**pecific - What exactly is the goal? Be as specific as possible.
- **M**easurable - Can you quantify it? Money, percentage, amounts?
- **A**ssignable - Who is going to do it?

- **R**ealistic - Can the results be achieved? Do we have enough and the right resources?
- **T**ime-related - When can the results be achieved?

SMART goal setting makes goals actionable, gives clarity and chances for achieving them increase.

Who else benefits?

When you make plans for achieving your goals, you do that for yourself, the team and the organisation. Very often, however, there are others who benefit as well. That makes them stakeholders. For them, as well as for you, it is interesting to know how they can benefit from your plans. If the benefits are big enough for them, they may actually help you reach your goals.

Have a look at your stakeholders analysis again. How powerful are they? How interested will they be? What will be your communication strategy? Are they able to free resources you can't?

If your plans are beneficial to others, you may have an extended team working on your goals. So, go analyse your plans and create synergy with these stakeholders!

Obstacles and pitfalls ahead!

There is always a reverse side of the medal. There will be stakeholders that will be less happy with your plans. How will you handle them?

Again your stakeholder analysis will help you. How powerful are they? How will they be affected by your plans? Will they actively try to prevent you from achieving your goals? How can and will they do that? Can you think of ways that make them benefit from your plans? Will they be willing to discuss

these possibilities? What are the win-wins?
Most projects and processes have pitfalls and obstacles.
That's also why you have to test your plans before you start
executing them. When problems have been anticipated, it's
much easier to switch to a plan B or C. You don't need to
"invent" problems, but it's also not wise to skip the
assessment.

What do you need to succeed.

There you are. You have just had your meeting with
your manager. He has handed over to you the set of annual
goals you have to achieve. A firm handshake, a pat on the
shoulder and a "good luck, you can do it" to finish the
meeting.
I hope this picture is not how you experience the annual goal
setting ritual. Hopefully, when you and your manager made
the plans, you also involved those who had to execute them.
Not only did you discuss *what* had to be achieved, but
certainly *how* as well. I have mentioned the word before. You
need *resources* to succeed.
What kind of resources do you need? That depends on the
goals or the project, but you can think in terms of
information, drawings, people, money, software, time, tools,
equipment, etc., etc. You can see it as the R in SMART. For
goals to be realistic, you need the right resources. Make sure
that you get the resources you really need or provide what
your team needs.

The House of Leadership

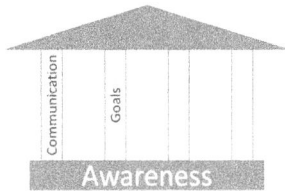

This chapter was mainly about goals, but we also continued working on awareness concerning stakeholder management and involving your team. We also dug a little deeper in the field of communication. Setting goals takes time, a lot of thinking and communication. There will be discussions, and goals have to be clarified. For many managers this is very difficult.

It is, however, very important to go through the process and plan ahead. This way, possible obstacles will be identified in an early stage and recognised when they appear. Failing to plan is planning for failure.

Don't forget to go to www.leadbetweenthelines.com/bonuses and download the bonuses I have ready for you. Use login code LBTL2014 to enter the page.

Chapter 8 - How do I tell them?

Make it or break it. Plan your communication.

When it comes down to being a successful leader, few skills are as important as communication. With consistent good communication and walking the talk, you can increase the level of trust in your environment. People can, however, also misplace or misinterpret your words. When you don't have the right feedback to correct the mistakes, the carefully built up trust evaporates.

In earlier chapters, I have already shown examples of planned communication. Remember the parts on stakeholder analysis and - management? How you first identified who they were and what their position towards you was? And that you then planned how you would communicate with each of them in a specific way?

Another example of planned communication is when you set your annual goals. You involve your team and discuss what is needed for the next year, consider plans to reach the goals and decide on resources.

Make it or break it. Miscommunication is one of the main reasons why things go wrong. One small miscommunication can start a full size conflict. Well planned communication on the other hand can bring in millions. Ever wondered why good copywriters earn fortunes in marketing? They are masters in communication, they know how words can trigger the desired emotions.

Think about what you want to achieve with your communication, before you actually start. What is the desired effect? What are the possible outcomes? What to do if an

undesired outcome occurs.
Think before you speak and save time, money and
frustrations.

Communication breakdown. The process.

The goal of effective communication is to send your
message clearly and unambiguously to one or more recipients.
In the last paragraph, I have explained that you should plan
your communication in order to be successful. The figure
below shows the process that will help you plan your
communication.

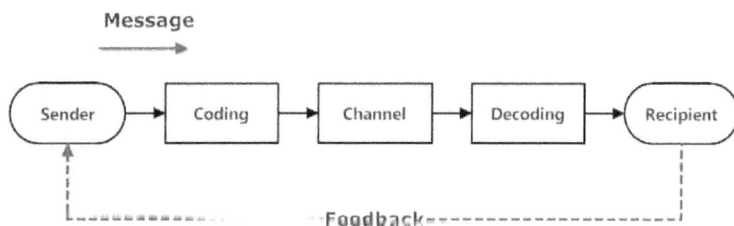

Imagine that you are the sender and you want to send a
message to a recipient. Before you do so, ask yourself some
open questions. What is it that I want to achieve with my
message? Do I want to inform or be informed? Who do I
want to inspire? Do I want to teach or coach them? What do
I tell them? Which items are not to be shared (yet)?
The next step is the coding of your message. How do you
wrap your message? What language is it in? Does it need to
have an emotional load? Do you need attributes to convey
the message better? Will you use pictures or can you paint
them with your story? Will it be in writing or is it a speech?
What will be the verbal and non-verbal parts enforcing the
message? Remember, at the other end, your message has to
be decoded by the recipient.

After coding, it's time to choose the right channel. Not all channels are equally suitable for all types of messages. What is it that needs to be achieved? What is your goal? Channels you can choose from are for instance: telephone, e-mail, instruction books, reports, television, Facebook, etc.

You should also be aware of the context you're making and sending your message in. How will the recipients be influenced by what's happening around them. How will your message add to that? How will the recipient feel? Is he happy or sad? Stressed or relaxed?

Let's switch roles. Now you are the recipient of a message. You have to "decode" the message that has been sent to you. What does that mean? Decoding is the interpretation of the message with the intention to actually understand what the message means. Decoding can be done in many ways, depending on the way the message has been coded. Listening, reading, sensing and looking are a few of them.

As a recipient, you consciously and unconsciously filter information and thus messages. You delete, distort or generalise them , depending on the state you're in. This has been researched by John Grinder and Richard Bandler and they came up with the NLP Communication Model (NLP = Neuro Linguistic Programming). When you search for this model on the internet, you will find an abundance of information. It's not very difficult and it will certainly help you to improve on how you communicate.

The behaviour shown by the recipient is the feedback for the sender. This is a very important part of the process, because it shows whether the message has been interpreted (decoded) correctly. At this point, the sender becomes the recipient.

The power of feedback

Imagine you did not get any feedback with regard to

your communication. How can you then know if the message
has landed as intended? You can't, can you? Anything can
happen with that message, it will start to lead a life of its own.
When you do get proper feedback about your message, you
will be able to see if there is a difference between what was
intended and what has been understood. Be aware that, since
you are the recipient now, you too filter the information fed
back to you. Feedback makes the communication process a
closed loop process.

When you know how your message has been interpreted, you
can, if necessary, make changes and go through the process
once more. You can make the changes in one or more
process steps. However, if you want to measure the results of
your changes, I would suggest to make one change at a time.
Repeat the cycle as often as necessary to make sure that the
message has been clearly and unambiguously understood.

Listen up

You have two ears and one mouth, so your listening
should be twice as good as your speaking. Good and
empathic listening is very difficult, and many managers and
leaders fail hopelessly.

Too many people listen in order to plan their reply, instead of
listening to really understand the other person. It takes
discipline not to interrupt or think about your reply. Make it a
habit to first try to understand before being understood. It is
one of the habits of highly effective leaders, that Dr. Stephen
R. Covey has explained in depth (habit 5 in his book The
Seven Habits of Highly Effective People).

Empathic listeners get new insights, find new ways to solve
issues and don't project their own scripts of life upon other
people's stories. Next time you're listening to someone, listen
in order to understand. Only ask questions that will help you

to better understand what is being said. A nice thing is, that when a person feels understood, that person will also try harder to understand you. Together you will arrive at better solutions than each of you could think of individually. Dr. Covey calls this "the third alternative".

Get them on board and on track

You can lead a horse to water, but you can't make it drink!

You can tell people what they have to do, but still they will decide for themselves if they will actually do it. To increase your chances that your plans will be executed, include the people responsible for the execution in your plan making. Do that in an early stage, so that they can contribute with their ideas. It will become their plan as well, and their commitment to it increases considerably.

If you have the right people to execute the plans, all you should do is facilitate them. Let go where possible and intervene where necessary. Let them own the project, but also let them report on the progress on a regular basis. Reward them for things well done, and help them where things can be improved. But beware not to push through your way of doing things. Listen emphatically, and jointly come to the right improvements.

Story telling

Which presenter gets your attention? The one with 185 PowerPoint slides (with ten bullet points per slide) or the one telling you a compelling story? I bet that it will be the latter. So why is it that there still are so many managers practising "death by PowerPoint"?

When you want to share your vision, plan and goals with a

group, don't start with creating a PowerPoint presentation.
First start with how you want to tell the story. What will they
see, hear, smell, experience when the goals are achieved? Take
them on your journey, make them part of your vision. What
does the world look like for those who have to execute or to
approve the plans? What's in it for them? Base your story on
them, not on yourself. If it is really necessary to make your
story stronger, you can still use PowerPoint slides. Just don't
make them boring and also don't make the PowerPoint
presentation the star of the show. It's there to support you,
not to remove you from the stage.
Use metaphors people can connect to, that are inspiring.
Show what can go wrong and how to avoid that. Show the
rewards when things go as planned. Inspire your audience.

Framing

When you are telling a good story, you paint a picture
in the minds of your audience. You share the details of the
scenery, so that the audience can enter that same scene as
well. You are framing your story. By doing so, you set the
boundaries of what you want to discuss or present.

Make that picture as clear as possible, as detailed as
possible. Everybody looks at your picture in his or her own
unique way. Everybody has his own set of experiences,
beliefs, values and attitudes to make their personal impression
of the picture you have painted. Just listen to the "after
meeting talks" and see how different the reactions from
different attendees are. By making your frame as detailed as
possible, the differences will be smaller.
Listen to the feedback you're getting to re-adjust the frame.

Handling fear

When you are presenting your plans, you must also take into consideration that your plans may impose fear on others. Fear comes with many faces:

- Fear of rejection
- Fear of failure
- Fear for the unknown
- Fear of loss
- Fear of conflict
- Fear of success
- Fear of change

Very often, those fears are unrealistic and have their roots in something that happened in the past. Mind you, the fear feels very realistic to the person experiencing it.

How do you handle fear? First find out where it comes from. Listen emphatically to others or yourself. Then, if you know where it has its roots, find the differences with the situation at hand. Find ways to overcome the fear. Remember that results from the past are no guarantee for the future. You and they have learnt from what happened then. Use those lessons to overcome fear and work your way forward.

Don't deny feelings of fear, but overcome them.

The House of Leadership

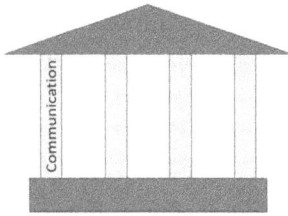

This was a chapter dedicated to communication. There were also parts relating to the foundation of awareness. Awareness for instance about how people filter information. Awareness of this phenomenon helps you to communicate more effectively. Good communication is crucial if you want to get to results. You have to practise a lot and be open when you're listening to others. Together you can make much more possible than on your own.

The next chapter will be dedicated to the execution pillar in the House of Leadership.

Chapter 9 - The power to achieve

Failing to plan is planning for failure

Not so long ago, I had the privilege of celebrating my fiftieth birthday. I won't bother you with my family history, but trust me, this was a milestone for me. I wanted to celebrate it big time. You can say I had a goal and it was SMART:

Specific: Celebrating my fiftieth birthday with family, good friends and close neighbours.

Measurable: I knew how many people I wanted to invite and who they were.

Assignable: My wife and I were going to organise it and we needed some help from my son and daughter.

Realistic: The resources were available and I had enough time to organise it.

Time related: Yep, my birthday!

The goal is clear. Does that mean it will miraculously happen? No, of course not. You will have to make plans. But how to do that? In my particular situation, celebrating my fiftieth birthday, I visualised what it would look like. I asked myself some questions to make the picture clearer. Who will be there? What activities do you want to happen? What will the weather be like? What food and drinks do you want to serve to the guests?

If you have made your mental picture, it's time to look back from that future. Imagine the steps you needed to take to make the picture happen. Who have you invited? Did you need to arrange a venue? Did you need the help of a caterer or did you take care of the food and drinks yourself? When and where did you do your shopping? What was on your shopping list? Which activities did you prepare?

For your own situation, after you have done this exercise, write down all the steps needed to achieve your (business) goals. It's not yet necessary to have them in a specific order. Just write down as many steps as you can think of. If you have them all written down, look into them in more detail. Which steps can be combined in clusters? Which are the big steps? Do they need to be broken down into smaller steps? When you have your work breakdown ready, estimate how much time and other resources the steps will consume. Now you can put the steps in a logical order. This is your plan. Put the steps in your planner and execute the plan!

If you don't have a plan yourself, you will become part of someone else's plan.

Managing resources

You know now which steps you have to take in order to achieve your goals. That's great. Now, look again at each step in your plan. What do you need to execute that specific step? How much time? How many people? What kind of people? Do you need special tools or material? Is it necessary to obtain financial resources? When do all the resources need to be available? Can you use some of the resources for other steps in the process as well?

As soon as you have all the answers on the resources, you can set up your complete plan and treat it as a project.

When you have major (annual) goals to achieve, I recommend you have a project list available. This gives you an overview on where you should have your focus. Derived from that, you can make short term "to-do" lists. By using them both, you can step by step progress towards achieving your goals. Make your progress visible and let it be your motivation to take the next steps.

Priorities

"What is important is seldom urgent and what is urgent is seldom important". It was former US president Dwight D. Eisenhower who said this and I think he is right. He used a matrix with four quadrants that helped him prioritise his busy work. I first learnt about this matrix through Stephen R. Covey. He used it in his book "The seven habits of highly effective people" and I think it's one of the strongest models I use in my daily life. The matrix helps you making a distinction between urgent and important and consists of four quadrants:

Q 1:   Important and urgent
Q 2:   Important but not urgent
Q 3:   Not Important but urgent
Q 4:   Not important and not urgent

Q1 tasks require immediate action and also work towards fulfilling long term goals and missions in life. Examples: crises, problems, deadlines.
Q2 tasks don't require immediate action, but are important to fulfil your long term goals and missions in life. Examples: strengthening relationships, self-development, planning.
Q3 tasks require immediate action (pressed upon us by others), but don't help us to achieve our long term goals or missions in life. Most of the time it helps those putting the pressure on achieving theirs. Examples: some phone calls, meetings and interruptions in general.
Q4 tasks are not important and not urgent. As such they should be avoided completely, but that's not always possible. Allow a maximum of 5 to 10% of your precious time for this

quadrant. Examples: watching soap series, aimlessly surfing on the internet and checking your smartphone every other minute.

As a rule of thumb:

    Q1 - Do it!
    Q2 - Plan it!
    Q3 - Delegate it!
    Q4 - Dump it!

Fighting or preventing fires?

Do you always want to work with pressing deadlines? Do you really need all that adrenaline rushing through your body? Go ahead, if you really want to. Keep working in Q1 and Q3 and see how long you will last. How long before the burnout? How long before your colleagues stop accepting your behaviour or your boss accepting your increasing portfolio of mistakes?

Yes, Q1 tasks need to be done. That's firefighting. But it shouldn't be your standard mode. Preventing fires is far more effective and far less expensive in many ways. Increase your time working in Q2, build good relationships, plan ahead and keep developing yourself and the people around you. When you take the time to plan ahead and do things correctly right the first time, you don't need the extra time to repair your mistakes afterwards. Investing in your preparation saves time and frustrations and increases quality.

Many busy people think they spend a lot of time in Q1, but what they are really doing is wasting that time in Q3. They don't allow themselves to take the time to reflect on what they are actually doing and as a result they don't achieve their goals. They are too busy doing the wrong things. Q3 is a giant pitfall. Realising this, and acting on it, will allow you to make giant steps towards reaching your goals. That what is important.

What has helped me in my career, was using my project- and to-do lists together with the matrix. I drew the matrix on a white board and used Post-it® to write down the issue and categorise it in the matrix. This is how simple the matrix can be:

	URGENT	NOT URGENT
IMPORTANT	I	II
NOT IMPORTANT	III	IV

An open culture for a clear view

In previous chapters I have explained that you're not on your own. There are many stakeholders interested in what you are doing. They have a certain power and can influence your results dramatically. And guess what, they have goals of their own as well. They too have stakeholders influencing their chances of success. They too did their planning and have agendas.

What do you prefer? Hidden or open agendas? Win-lose or win-win? At least within your own organisation it's very important to have an open culture. That's why I have advised you to involve your team in goal setting and making the plans to achieve them. When you know each other's goals and the overall goals of the organisation, you know what is important and what is just urgent.

Knowing each other's goals, makes asking for assistance also more effective. You can ask yourself: "Is what I'm asking also important for the person I'm asking it? If not, who am I going to ask then? Or should I make it important for that person?"

Can you see the power of an open culture and a clear view on the goals? Unfortunately, for many organisations this isn't common practice. Internal battles take place, goals are not reached, resulting in heavy losses and ultimately in bankruptcy.

If people forget what is important, help them to remind. If they come with requests that are not important (for you), say no. If it is important for them and you know who can help them, redirect them.

Keep your eyes on the road, your hands on the wheel

Your goals are clear and so is your planning. You know what you need to succeed and to work towards achieving your goals. But do you know how much progress you have made and if you are on track? You have to know where in the process you are, you have to keep track of your progress on all your important projects and goals.

Where are you now? Where do you want to get to? What is the gap? Which steps do you need to take to close the gap? Being active with your projects- and to-do lists will continuously give you the insights needed. Make it a habit to have different levels in your planning: short, medium and long term plans.

Too often, at the end of the year, the year plan is dusted off. Just to find out that most goals haven't been achieved and that the majority of the available time has been spent in firefighting mode. A strange thing about this, is that when managers are confronted with this, they still believe they have done a great job extinguishing fires. I wonder if they realise that most of those fires have been the result of them not planning and keeping track of their goals. They may have worked hard, but not very effectively.

Walk your talk

One of the best ways to build trust is to say what you do and to do what you say. In other words, walk your talk. When you're making sure that the plans are executed, you make promises to yourself and others. Be sure that you also keep your promises. Not doing so will destroy the trust people have in you and it will be very hard to keep your team motivated.
Sometimes you don't even realise you have promised something. You may not have explicitly promised it, but people might have interpreted it as such. If this happens a lot, evaluate your communication. Did you get certain feedback that indicated some disappointment about you not keeping promises? You might need to give some more attention to your communication. You have to manage the expectations.

Be yourself. There are already plenty of others.

At the end of chapter one, I wrote a paragraph in which I asked you if you felt overwhelmed. We are much further now and I wonder if you feel overwhelmed by now or that you have found the answers you have been looking for. Feel free to leave a message on the Facebook page (www.facebook.com/leadbetweenthelines), Amazon.com or

the website www.leadbetweenthelines.com.
You have already gone through a lot of information and
certainly when this is your first book on leadership and you
haven't had much practice yet, it will be overwhelming.
Remember that you don't have to implement everything at
once. Take your time, practise and dare to ask assistance.
In that process you will change, you will grow. Learn from
others without copying them one on one. Give it your own
personal touch. Be yourself, be authentic. Most people don't
like non-authentic leaders and can smell them right away.
Being authentic doesn't mean that you always, under all
circumstances, act the same. There are many versions of you
in you and they can all be authentic. The happy you will be
totally different from the sad you, but it is still you. Be
yourself and stay yourself during the process and learn how to
behave under circumstances for which you have not found
the right behaviour yet.

The House of Leadership

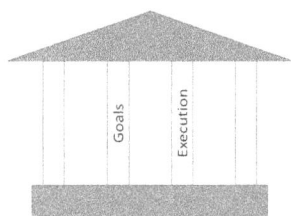

We have touched the foundation, all pillars and the roof in this chapter. However, the emphasis was on goals and execution. They were supported by the foundation of awareness and accompanied by the pillars of communication and learning. The open culture and clear view are elements of the roof of trust.

In the next chapter we will continue with the pillar of learning.

Don't forget to go to www.leadbetweenthelines.com/bonuses. I have free bonuses waiting for you on goal setting and goal getting, as well as on prioritising and the House of Leadership. Use LBTL2014 as your login code to enter the page.

Chapter 10 - Lifelong learning

The risk of education

Don't you agree that it's a bit odd that there are organisations that regard education of their employees as a luxury? They may not say so, but one of the first budgets to be cut when the going gets tough, is the one for training, coaching and mentoring.

When they are hiring people, they look at the level of education the candidates have received in the past (schools, universities, former employers). After the hiring, only a small budget for further education will be available. And these funds will mainly be used for mandatory training for the first line workforce. Investment in management training and - coaching will only be done when there is trouble in paradise. It's a reactive approach and therefore it's lagging behind.

What exactly is the risk of education? Will your employees become too smart for your business? Are you afraid they will ask for higher salaries when they have a higher level of education? Will it hurt your bottom line?

This may all be good reasons for the short term if you're financially challenged, but certainly not for the long haul. Unfortunately, for many organisations that have struggled to make ends meet, this has become a habit. It's now their long term vision. They don't realise that their top players want to grow further. They also don't realise that they lose ground to their competitors, who do train their employees.

Fortunately there are many organisations as well that do have a proper budget for learning. These organisations understand that the world is changing continuously and at a rapid pace.

They have a proactive approach towards learning and take care that their employees remain fit for their tasks. They even train their high potentials for their next level.
How about your organisation? How do they value education? Is that in line with your ideas?

The costs of failing to educate

Yep! You may think that after you have trained your employees, they will either ask for a raise or leave the company. That can happen. But what happens if you don't keep your workforce fit for purpose? Your innovative power drops and thus your competitive power. People who want to be educated, which are probably those that can help your organisation grow, will leave. This leaves you with those that don't want to be educated anymore. Is that a pretty sight? When one of your better managers or leaders leaves the company because he has been denied proper training, who is going to fill the gap? Will the next one be prepared for his job or is everyone going to watch him struggle and stumble?
What does not educating your employees mean for:
1 . The motivation of those that do want to be trained?
2 . The competitive power of the company?
3 . The attractiveness for new employees?
4 . The attractiveness for new customers?
5 . The leadership skills of the management?
6 . Your profit?
7 . Your sustainability?
Cutting costs on education can be done, but be careful where you do that. Cut costs on those initiatives that don't add value to the organisation or its goals. Don't think too light on what added value actually means for you, your team, your organisation.

Survival, the strongest or the fittest?

Good old Mr. Darwin figured it out quite well. It was the survival of the fittest, not necessarily the strongest. The very strong dinosaurs went extinct about sixty-five million years ago. In business however, they still exist! But for how long will they last? If they don't go extinct, the companies containing too many of them will.

But how do you stay fit and prevent your company from going extinct? Quite simple, keep learning! On all levels and in all disciplines. Stay on the edge!

The world is changing at an incredible speed and won't wait for those left behind. Markets come and go, as do companies. Big names from the past don't exist anymore. Complete industries vanished. Nowadays getting information on almost everything has become relatively simple. What is new today is history tomorrow.

You, your team, your organisation, all of you have to continue updating yourselves. By training, by coaching or mentoring, by reading books, following blogs of thought leaders, by actively being involved in online discussions, etc. Get out of the office and meet the world!

In addition, make sure that the learning is not only on an individual level. Capture the collective learnings in systems and share knowledge and skills. Keep on learning together, keep in shape, stay fit and stay in business.

The fittest will survive, but it takes discipline to stay the fittest!

How we learn

How do you learn? Do you like to read a lot and make summaries? Or do you rather like to draw pictures or doodles of what you have read? Maybe you like to be told or shown how to do things? Or even better, you do it and the teacher watches.

There are many ways you can learn, and it's up to you to pick the method that suits you best for that particular situation. Generally spoken, the best way to learn is by doing. People tend to forget what they have learnt rather quickly. Repeating the lessons frequently and quickly after you have learnt them, helps to ingrain it in your brain.

Another way to look at how we learn is by using the Mastery Cycle. It shows four phases in you learning new skills.

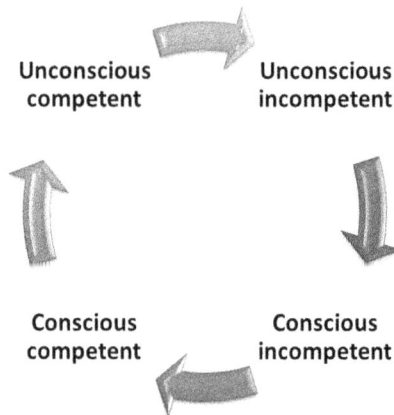

Unconscious competent   Unconscious incompetent

Conscious competent   Conscious incompetent

- Unconscious incompetent. You're not yet aware that you miss a certain skill. For instance, you don't know you need leadership skills.
- Conscious incompetent. You have become aware that you miss a certain skill. You have been offered a leadership position and realise you have to learn new skills.
- Conscious competent. You are busy learning and you have acquired the skill. However you still have to think through the steps. You have learnt technical leadership skills, but you're still a bit uncertain in using them.

- Unconscious competent. You have mastered the skill. You don't have to think about each step, you know what you're doing. You're now a seasoned leader, handling your tasks with ease and confidence.

Training and coaching

Some people think that after finishing school, they have finished learning. How wrong can you be. Most of your learning will be done after you have left school behind. Keep your mind open towards learning and for certain you will achieve much more than those who have stopped learning. When someone is offered a leadership position, he should first have had a good leadership training. It is still more common that people are plunged into leadership and that does a lot of harm to many. When someone is promoted to a new level, he must be prepared.

After having had training and starting in the new position, the new leader should be coached and mentored in order to make the transition as smooth as possible for everybody involved.

Training is for teaching new skills.

Mentoring happens when the mentor shares his experience to help the new leader in his position.

With *coaching* the coach challenges the coachee with questions. A good coach takes a person where he can't take himself.

A good coach is:

Committed
Objective
Accountable
Challenging
Helpful

If you are in a leadership position, get yourself a good coach (internal or external) and make sure you get trained on a regular basis. You cannot afford to lag behind.

The learning organisation

Organisations can keep themselves fit by providing training and coaching to their employees on all levels. But there are far more ways in which organisations can learn. A very important one is collective learning from the activities within the organisation.

You set goals, make plans to achieve them and execute the plans. If it would stop here, there wouldn't be much learning involved. It makes sense to evaluate the process afterwards. What are the lessons learnt? Which parts will you do the same next time? Where do you need to improve? What exactly and how? Can more departments or individuals learn from your experiences?

Evaluate the processes with the people involved and, when useful, also invite experts from other departments. Be soft on the people and hard on the matter. The evaluation is important feedback for future activities. When new projects are to be started, intelligent companies, teams and leaders first collect lessons learnt from previous projects. It may take some extra time in the preparation, but that will be won back in the execution phase. Intelligent organisations also have systems available in which they share all experiences within (and frequently also outside) the organisation. In other words Plan Do Check Act

One plus one is...

...whatever you want to make of it.

If people are actually working together and share in order to grow, the outcome can be beyond imagination. If, on the other hand, people keep all information to themselves, the outcome will be negative. Some people think knowledge is power and keep that knowledge to themselves. Shared knowledge is much more powerful and will also help the person who has shared it to advance.

When people are open and willing to share amongst each other, magic can and will happen. To make this possible there must be an atmosphere of trust. People must feel free and comfortable to share. If they receive negative comments or feel ignored or not heard, they will stop sharing.

What can you do to promote sharing? If it is not yet common practice within your organisation, be the first to start. Create a safe environment, free of premature judgement and start sharing yourself. Discuss mistakes you have made, dare to be vulnerable, but also share your successes and successes of your team. Compliment them on their achievements. Help others to learn together by facilitating the sharing process.

As soon as other people see the results coming, they will be curious and start sharing themselves as well. Watch the power you have released and enjoy the ride!

A last remark: don't let yourself be held back by negativism of other people! Some people just don't want you to be successful. Don't allow them to be your anchor.

The House of Leadership

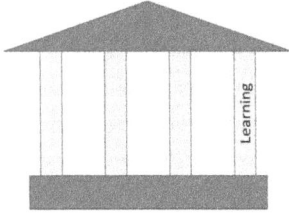

This chapter was all about the pillar of learning. Often underestimated, but incredibly important. If your organisation fails to learn, it will vanish.

If you find yourself in an environment full of politics, try to change that step by step in order to rescue it. If you think you're too small for that, imagine you are a mosquito in a bedroom. Imagine two people in that warm room, who are almost asleep. Now you start buzzing. What happens? Would you see change? The same goes for you in your organisation, start buzzing...

Chapter 11 - Building trust

Character and competencies

What comes to your mind when you think about trust? Is it the nice person, you can trust? The one with a high integrity and good intentions? The modest but courageous guy? Yes, these character traits are part of a trustworthy person. But there is more that makes you decide if you can trust a person.

Think of a loved one close to you and who you trust blindly. Would you trust that person to do a heart surgery on you? With very few exceptions, most of you will immediately say "NO!". Why? Because here the second part of trust comes in place: competencies. So, whether or not you trust a person depends on that person's character and the competencies needed for a certain situation. The good news is, both can be trained and improved. The sad news is, both can be destroyed as well.

Time and money

In his book "The Speed of Trust" Stephen M.R. Covey explains there is a time and money factor to the level of trust. When trust is going down, costs and time spent are going up. When trust improves, costs and time spent go down. Interesting isn't it? Think about your team or organisation. Can you speak freely? Do you have meetings where nobody contributes or where there are just a few people battling to make their point? Do you need to make large contracts with the help of a legal team to sell your products or services? What are the costs? How much time do you need to spend on this? What if you could increase the level of trust? What would be the results?

An interesting and simple to understand example of how ruined trust costs a lot of money and time, is the time we are living in now, after the 9/11 attacks on the Twin Towers in 2001.

Billions have been invested in security on airports, in ports and intelligence. The time needed to go through all procedures before a plane can take off has increased dramatically as well. In his book, Stephen M.R. Covey brings a lot of research and examples to the table and also shows ways to improve on trust. I highly recommend you to read this book and see what you can do to improve yourself, your team, your organisation, your industry and society in general. As I have mentioned before, you can make a difference!

Who to trust?

How about starting with yourself on this one? Just like we did with your leadership. If you can't lead yourself, how can you expect to lead others? If you can't trust yourself, how can you expect to trust others? Or how can you expect others to trust you?

Why is it that you can't trust yourself? Have you made yourself too small? Or have you let other people do that to you? Do you lack confidence? Don't you have the right competencies? For what? If you don't trust yourself, get over it and work on your improvement! Is it your character or are your competencies holding you back? Find out what it is and focus on improvement. Talk to people. Ask them to be honest with you, let them help you find your blind spots. Not only the things that need improvement, but also those positive blind spots. Discover that you have a lot of strong points and use them to build confidence.

When you have dealt with yourself, look at your relationships.

Who do you trust and why? Is it character or competencies or both? In your professional environment, which stakeholders do you trust and which not? Why don't you trust them? What have they done to lose your trust? How important is that particular relationship? Is there anything you can do to restore the level of trust with that person? What does a restored relationship mean in terms of time, money or opportunities?

Now look one step further. How is your company or industry perceived? Does your company conduct business with integrity? Are there scandals surrounding your industry or your company? How come? Is this an environment you want to work in? What is your contribution?

Hard to build, easy to lose

What do you need to build trust? You need to be...trustworthy! You must be worth being trusted. But how do you become trustworthy? You build, or destroy, trustworthiness by your behaviour. Are you straightforward? Do you inform the people around you? Do you walk your talk? Do you treat people with respect? Are you loyal? These are all traits building your character. It's about who you are and what you do.

Now take a piece of paper and divide it in two columns. In one column you write the name of a person you trust completely and in the other a person you don't trust at all. Now, below those names you write down all the reasons why you trust or distrust that particular person.

What have you found? Behaviour? What can you learn from this? What behaviours do you show yourself? Which build trust in you and which bring it down? If you want to build trust, you must work on your trustworthiness by working on good behaviours and saying goodbye to the bad ones. Work on your character as well as on your competencies. And by the way – make sure you don't leave this piece of paper lying around!

Managing expectations

Have you ever been disappointed in someone? What caused that disappointment? What did it do to you and the relationship with that person? Disappointment comes from not meeting expectations. Very often the person causing the disappointment isn't even aware of the disappointment he causes or the expectations you had of him.

In our communication with others, we, consciously or unconsciously, build expectations. If you want to avoid disappointment, it's important to know what expectations others have of you. This way you can manage these expectations.

Your manager, for instance, may expect you to make a profit of $10,000.- in February. You, however, know in January that one of your clients has postponed or cancelled a big order. This will result in a $10,000.- loss instead of a profit. What are you going to do? Tell your boss or wait until March when the February figures will be available? When you want to build trust, you'd better tell him right away. This way he knows upfront, and maybe together you can find alternatives to realise a $10,000.- profit anyway.

Managing expectations is all about clarity, and is a solid trust builder. Be open and clear to your team, yourself, your boss and your organisation. Not only when things tend to go wrong, but also when positive deviations occur.

Trust and communication

As you undoubtedly have understood from the previous paragraph, trust is greatly enhanced by good communication. Be aware of the signals you give. Be a conscious communicator and plan your communication (we have seen that one before). Be sensitive to feedback. What message are they sending? Can you distillate expectations they may have and of which you are not yet aware? Listen to understand, not in order to defend. If they have misunderstood your message, adjust the message and thus the expectations.

Share what is sharable and hold back what is confidential. Stay away from gossip and promote open conversations. Help others to improve their communication as well. Explain the benefits of increased trust to them. Remember, the higher the trust, the less time and money is wasted.

Gut feeling and facts

Feelings are true. At least for the person experiencing them. As I have explained in the chapter about communication, we all filter information. And we all filter it differently. No wonder that we often disagree on what we feel are facts. We just process information differently.

There are people that always trust their gut feeling and maybe you are one of them. Now that you know that everybody filters information, you can also understand that gut feeling can be based on incomplete information. Therefore it's advisable to double check your gut feeling before you make decisions. It can save you lots of time, money and frustrations.

Clever salesmen know that people buy on emotion and justify it with ratio. With that knowledge, they know how to stimulate the gut feeling in their advantage and will supply the facts to feed the ratio as well.

If you're acting on gut feeling most of the time, take a time-out every now and then to test that gut feeling. Find the facts before you make a decision. If the facts really support your gut feeling, go ahead and make the decision. If not, be glad you took a time-out.

The House of Leadership

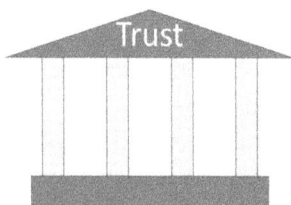

In this chapter we have placed the roof of trust on our House of Leadership. I hope you will make it a strong one. Trust as much as you can without becoming naive. Be a great communicator and listen to understand. Listen to your gut feeling, but test it with facts.

Save money and time by being trustworthy!

Chapter 12 - What's next?

Should I stay or should I go?

Congratulations! You have made it to the last chapter! I hope I have given you enough food for thought. What do you think of leadership now? Is the picture I have painted helping you to continue or has it caused you to stop? Is this what you want to do for the rest of your career, climbing the ladder step by step? If you have really read all the previous chapters, I'm pretty sure that you are committed and want to continue on your journey into leadership.

For me it has been and still is an exciting journey. I love it when every day brings new challenges. I love to develop people and organisations beyond what they think is possible. I enjoy it when I see what great leaders can create by utilising (hidden) capabilities of their followers. I hope that by now you share this feeling and I sincerely hope you will utilise your power to build greatness in yourself and in others.

If (formal) leadership isn't "your thing", that's fine too. Contribute in another way. Do what you're good at and what gives you energy. You can still build greatness in yourself and others. One way or another, you're always a leader. To the very least, you lead the life you live. Make it worth living!

Preparing for the future

What is the future? Is it a dot at the horizon or the journey towards that dot and beyond? For me it's the latter. Your future starts now and only ends when you're dead and no longer remembered. How do you prepare for that? That depends. What do you want your future to look like? Some parts of your future are destined to be, but there's also a big part that you can shape yourself.

If you have a clear picture of what you want to achieve, you can make plans and execute them. If you don't have a picture yet, start thinking about it, or become part of someone else's plan. Focus on those things you can influence and see your influence grow. Develop yourself by reading, training, coaching, mentoring and communicating. If you teach others, you will find that your learning also improves.

Everybody will encounter difficulties in life. It's how you handle those difficult periods that shapes you. The better you prepare yourself, the better you will handle all situations.

Books to read

There are and have been many great leadership authors. The suggestions I have assembled for you are far from complete and you may miss authors you think should have been mentioned. I apologise upfront.

For me, the most important leadership author is by far Dr. Stephen R. Covey. His book, "The Seven Habits of Highly Effective People" has influenced and helped millions of leaders and their followers worldwide. In my opinion, all his books are well worth reading, but I strongly suggest to start with "The Seven Habits of Highly Effective People".

When you want to learn more about trust, read his son's book "The Speed of Trust".

How to lead in different situations is best described by Dr. Paul Hershey in his book "Situational Leadership".

Do you want to increase your influence? Then Robert B. Cialdini is the go-to guy. His book "Influence. Science and practice" is the result of his lifelong research into the field of influence. His book is widely adapted by marketers. But of course you understand that marketing is not the only area where you would benefit from an increased level of influence.

The master on self-development is Anthony Robins. His book "Unlimited Power, the New Science of Personal Achievement" helps you to understand and improve yourself. Anthony Robins frequently performs on stage, with highly energetic seminars. If you ever have the chance, attend one. It may change your life.

Having difficulties getting everything done? David Allen wrote "Getting Things Done". The title is self-explanatory and together with the Eisenhower Matrix, his system will help you to really get your things done.

Curious about the blueprints of companies? Read "Business Model Generation" by Alexander Osterwalder & Yves Pigneur. A revolutionary book, co-created with 470 practitioners from 45 different countries.

Interested in achieving your goals? Eliyahu M. Goldratt and Jeff Cox wrote "The Goal". A business book disguised as a novel, explaining the theory of constraints. A pleasure to read and very insightful.

In my chapter on communication, I have mentioned empathic listening. Daniel Goleman wrote "Emotional Intelligence". Ground-breaking, and it gave me the insight why certain leaders with a high IQ failed so miserably in getting results.

The master on thinking is Edward de Bono. His book "Six Thinking Hats" gives you tools when you have to make tough decisions. Don't miss it, it can also improve the way you conduct meetings.

If you wonder which role everyone in your team plays, read "Team Roles at Work" By R. Meredith Belbin. He explains the different characters and what that means for the structure of your team.

The last, but certainly not the least book I want to advise, is "Maverick" by Ricardo Semler. He revolutionised leadership within his company Semco. He is an example for many other companies. Written in 1993 and still cutting edge!

Other resources

Apart from books, there are many other resources helping you to enhance your leadership. You can think of training, mentoring or coaching for instance. Online or offline.

With my company, Trainnovation (www.trainnovation.nl/), I help leaders in an industrial environment. This is offline. Online I have a membership site exclusively for the Dutch market. Translated it's called Lessons in Leadership, and I help starting and struggling leaders to get control over their leadership. It can be found on www.lesseninleiderschap.nl. Online, you will also find many blogs of thought leaders and leadership authors. Google your favourite author and find out about his blog. Most of the times you can register for regular updates.

On the website of this book (www.leadbetweenthelines.com) I will also place blogposts.

Other important resources can be found in your direct environment, within your own organisation. Ask your peers and leaders for their experiences. Nine out of ten will gladly share them with you.

Bonuses

As it says on the front cover, this book comes with four bonuses. I have mentioned them several times in different chapters.

For sake of completeness, here they are once more:

1. A free MP3 audio file about the House of Leadership.
2. A free PDF, "10 steps to better goal setting and goal getting".
3. A free video on prioritising.
4. 50% off on a brain preference assessment, including an

intake and personal advice by me.

To collect and enjoy the bonuses go to
www.leadbetweenthelines.com/bonuses and enter the page
logging in with LBTL2014. I'm sure you'll like them.

Share your experience

Share as much as you can! I've said it many times.
Together you will learn so much more than on your own and
it's much more fun. I would like to ask you to share your
impressions of this book. Share them with people you know
can benefit from it. Help them to stop suffering, to start
leading and to get results. I would also like to ask you to share
your experiences online, on my website, the Facebook page
or at Amazon.com. Maybe somewhere in the world someone
picks up your signal and is helped by your comments.
I firmly believe in growing by sharing.

Thank you!

It was with great pleasure writing this book. And I
hope that it was with great pleasure that you have read it.
The book has been on my wish list (or to-do list) for many
years and now that I am writing my final lines, a feeling of
gratitude comes over me.
Thank you for reading the book and I wish you all the best in
your career as a leader!

's-Gravendeel
The Netherlands
July 25th. 2014

Acknowledgements

This book has been in me for such a long time and now finally I can share it all with you. I'm feeling very grateful for that and I know I can't personally thank all those who have made this possible.

However, I want to thank some people who have contributed to this book by name.

First I want to thank my wonderful wife, Anja, who has endured me for over 25 years now. She has always been a tremendous support for me.

I want to thank my parents, Hanneke and Dirk, who have always been there when I needed them. They supported me in my choices, both privately and professionally. They took care that I could build a solid basis.

My daughter Thalassa. Thank you for your detailed advise and corrections in my writing. Without you, the book would not have the quality it has now.

My son Dexter. Thank you for your part in making the pictures look better and for your enthusiastic support on social media.

I also want to thank Allison Newell and Koen Zonneveld for their part in enhancing my spelling, grammar and style.

Thank you Gaia Nuissl of Gaialab for designing my covers and advising me on design in general.

Thank you Raymond Aaron and Lori Murphy for your support in the whole writing process and for offering me your 10-10-10 program. Without this program, I would not have started and the book would still remain in my head only.

And last but not least, a thank you for all those people I have interacted with in my professional life. These interactions, whether they were positive or negative, have built my experience and knowledge on the subject of leadership.

www.ingramcontent.com/pod-product-compliance
Lightning Source LLC
Chambersburg PA
CBHW060625210326
41520CB00010B/1471